The TT Races

A Photographic History

RAYMOND AINSCOE

Published in 2007 by Ilkley Racing Books
3 Mendip House Gardens Curly Hill Ilkley LS29 0DD

The TT Races: A Photographic History: ISBN 978 0 9524802 3 9

Printed by The Amadeus Press, Cleckheaton, West Yorkshire

Editor in chief: Stewart Clague

Dedicated to the unsung heroes: the scrutineers, marshals and volunteers without whose efforts the TT races could not be run.

Front cover: Joey Dunlop, Honda Britain RC30, 1993. In keeping with our usual policy for cover shots, the photo was taken at Quarter Bridge. Joey Dunlop was truly a remarkable man: think not simply of his haul of 26 TT victories but also of his ventures to Romanian orphanages, filling his van with food and blankets, and crossing borders by bribing corrupt guards with stickers and magazines.

INTRODUCTION

As we stand on the verge of the centenary of the TT, it gives me great pleasure to welcome you to this photographic history of the world-famous event.

S.C.S., a Manx company trading for nearly forty years, was delighted when approached with the opportunity to sponsor this illustrated record of the course, the men and the machines which together have contributed to the legend of the world's greatest road races.

As a Manxman, I have been fortunate enough to have witnessed and enjoyed almost six decades of the races but, for personal reasons, we at S.C.S. have never sponsored individual riders. We do, however, recognise the part played in the Island's life by the TT and are pleased that all profits from the sale of the book will be donated to The Rob Vine Fund.

To those of you who intend to visit the Isle of Man, remember that the Island has much more to offer than the TT festival.

It is an island steeped in history, and boasting areas of outstanding natural beauty. I invite you to visit the Ballannette nature reserve which S.C.S. sponsors. Please look us up on our website at www.scs.co.im and we hope to see you on the Island soon.

Warmest regards,

Stewart Clague, M.D.
S.C.S. Limited, Baldrine,
December 2006

An unusual shot of Ballacraine, with the famous monkey puzzle tree to the left of the hotel. The hotel has been closed for some years but the famous landmark and the tree remain. Contrary to the usually recounted anecdote, the Slagdyke Daredevil, George Shuttleworth, did not crash through the hotel's front door in "No Limit"; the unfortunate rider who did so was one of his rivals. Incidentally, the classic film contains some marvellous shots of the course. Filming took place in the summer of 1935. Director Monty Banks approached the Peveril Motorcycle and Light Car Club which provided a group of stunt riders, including the brothers Bertie and Harold Rowell and Jack Cannell who together went on to win the club team prize at the Manx GP in 1937. Some of the comedy scenes were genuine; when George came down from Douglas Head on Granpa's trike, he really did biff the local bobby, who was not amused. And when he collapsed in a heap with his Rainbow at the finishing line, it was no act; it was a hot day, and numerous "takes" as he pushed the bike along Glencrutchery Road had taken their toll on the chimney sweep's assistant.

ACKNOWLEDGEMENTS

Stewart has mentioned that the TT is about so much more than the races themselves. As a schoolboy, I was fortunate to be taken to the Isle of Man for TT week on many occasions; my memories are not simply of watching my heroes from the outside banking or inner wall at Quarter Bridge but also of all the complementary features - the BP booklets of the previous year's races, the free Castrol film show (at which Castrol Achievements booklets, transfers and flags were handed out to the eager young fans), buying "The TT Special" for the same day race reports, getting the early morning bus up to the Creg while clutching the obligatory packed lunch from our b&b (the Pitcairn), the annual visit to howl at Speed Demon George Formby (Shuttleworth Snap and Rainbow) in the classic "No Limit" - recollections which so many readers will share.

Nevertheless, the races were, and indeed remain, the central attraction. In assembling the photographs which you will find within these pages, we sought primarily illustrations of the famous stretches of Manx roads which make the TT a unique challenge for the rider and spectacle for the fan.

In selecting the (appropriate) one hundred photographs, I have been fortunate to have been assisted by Elwyn Roberts, who boasts a virtually unrivalled knowledge of the photographic history of the TT - not to mention a wonderful archive. If credits are not given for the photographs in this book, they are most likely from Elwyn's archive or from my collection. (Every effort has been made to trace copyright owners. If by any mischance, we have omitted to give credit, the copyright owner is invited to contact the publisher.)

I am also very grateful for the help given by Walter Radcliffe of Ramsey, a long-serving marshal, supporter and sponsor of the races. This book could not have appeared without the help of Manx residents Bill Snelling of FoTTofinders, Tony Breese of Racing Photos IOM and Eddy Richardson. Thanks are also due to the legendary Peter Murray of Santon not only for the provision of photographs but also for his TT anecdotes, garnered from numerous summers as the proprietor of what was, in my opinion, the world's best museum, situated for so many years at the Bungalow.

Thanks also to my wife Elizabeth and our children, all of whom have willingly shared countless holidays in the Island, during TT and Manx GP fortnights. And last but not least, this book has its origins in the prompting and support of Barbara and Stewart Clague and their colleagues at S.C.S. Limited. I owe them a big "thank you" not only for their sponsorship of this book but also for their marvellous Manx hospitality in Baldrine.

Raymond Ainscoe, Ilkley, December 2006

The author and his father pictured outside the Ballacraine Hotel, TT week 1964.

The winner of the Single-cylinder class of the first TT, in 1907, was Charlie Collier (Matchless) - arguably the TT's first "man to beat". He covered the 158 miles in 4 hours, 8 minutes and 8 seconds at 38.22 mph. Collier was runner-up in 1908 and won again in 1910 when we see him at Glen Wyllin, near Kirkmichael. Collier's great rival was Triumph's Jack Marshall who was runner-up to him in 1907 but reversed the tables in the following year. When asked to describe the roads, Marshall explained "Mud-covered and slippery in the wet; very dusty in the dry. In an attempt to damp down the dust, the officials sprayed the course with an acid solution which was supposed to keep things moist. The acid got on to our clothes and in a couple of days they looked as if the rats had been at them!"

(Walter Radcliffe collection)

The scene of the start and finish of the short course at St John's; the 1910 event gets underway. Although cars had been racing over a Mountain course in the Island since 1904, the motorcycles were incapable of coping with the slopes of Snaefell (Norse for snow mountain) and so, for the first four editions, the TT was held over the 15½ miles of the triangular St John's course.

Starting at the village green in St John's, the riders headed to Ballacraine, where a wooden banking was erected on the exit as a so-called safety feature; movie film exists of riders attempting this "Wall of Death" - most simply fell off. The riders headed north to Kirkmichael, then turned sharp left at Douglas Road Corner. Following the coast road, the riders came to, and rode through, Peel before heading back to St John's to complete the lap. Celebrated features of the course included Creg Willey's Hill (the "mountain" of the "short course", on which the rider often had to leap off his steed and run alongside it) and the Devil's Elbow on the coast road.

(Walter Radcliffe collection)

Harry Reed, the founder of the Dot firm and winner of the Twin-cylinder class in 1908, rides one of his machines through Peel in the 1910 race, the last TT over the St. John's course - because the machines were said to be "too fast for the course" (with the lap record set at 53.15 mph by H.H. Bowen, B.A.T.). Reed was in fourth place until lap four of the ten, when the belt jammed and broke the pulley. (See "Devoid of Trouble: The story of Dot Motorcycles 1903 -1978" by Ted Hardy, published in 1998.)

Harry Collier (Matchless) rounds Douglas Road Corner, Kirkmichael, turning south towards Peel in the 1910 race in which he was runner-up to brother Charlie. Harry boasts plate number one in honour of his victory in 1909. Harry was again runner-up in 1911, in the Junior category. It was their father who founded the Matchless concern in 1899. *(Walter Radcliffe collection)*

1911 and the TT moved to the Mountain circuit - very similar to today's course, save for some minor variation in Ramsey and that the riders turned right at Cronk-ny-Mona and arrived at Parkfield Corner before turning right to plunge down Bray Hill. The famous Senior and Junior categories were introduced and it was no longer permissible to push or wheel the machine against the race direction (and see Mike Hailwood, 1965, as to that!). The Rudge team of 1911 is pictured at its base, the Glen Helen Hotel. Nearest the camera was Victor Surridge who tragically became the event's first fatality. He crashed in practice just outside the hotel, beneath the horrified gaze of the team manager, Mr Holroyd (standing to the left in the photo). The squad was withdrawn as a mark of respect.

An unidentified rider passes through Kirkmichael in one of the pre-Great War Mountain course races.

Jacob (popularly Jake) De Rosier was Indian's crack board track rider and led the American team's attack on the Senior TT in 1911. When asked if he had any strategy for the race, he replied, "Yep, I aim to learn the course thoroughly - in the dark. There's no better way. For one thing, you're not distracted by the scenery and, for another, once you've learned the course by the light of the moon and the stars - why it's just a cinch when you ride it in broad daylight."

"It ain't gonna be no tea party," he quipped. Here we see him at Stella Maris. He surged ahead of Charlie Collier but the Matchless ace passed his rival on the second lap. In the chase the Yank fell heavily and was subsequently disqualified from 12th place for receiving outside assistance.

However, De Rosier's team-mates Godfrey, Franklin and Moorhouse registered a stunning one-two-three for the Indian raiders. What happened to Collier? He actually finished in second place but, following a protest by Messrs Franklin and Moorhouse, he was disqualified for taking on petrol at a point other than a recognised control. There were official pits in both Ramsey and Douglas.

The start of the 1913 races at Woodlands, Quarter Bridge Road. We can identify A. Bashall (25, Douglas) and W. Heaton (42, AJS), competitors in the Junior event, and C. Franklin (129) and A.H. Alexander (88), Indian teamsters in the Senior class. The Juniors were to wear blue 'waistcoats' and do two laps on the Wednesday morning; the Seniors, kitted out in red bibs, would do three laps in the afternoon. The survivors, or 75% of the starters if fewer, would start together on the Friday, completing four more laps.

(Walter Radcliffe collection)

The 1913 Junior: T. Thompson (Douglas) leaving Parliament Square and the replenishment pits in Ramsey.

(Walter Radcliffe collection)

The Senior TT of 1913 was won by a rider appearing in his first race. H. O. Wood was Scott's tester; he and brother Clarence, another stalwart of Scott lore, had been educated at Bradford Technical College where H. O. was known, for obvious reasons, as "Timber", abbreviated to Tim. Younger brother Clarrie duly became "Splinters".

At the conclusion of the Wednesday instalment, Wood held a lead of 4 seconds over Rudge's young star Bateman. At the re-start two days later, Wood encountered problems; a flying stone cut a water pipe obliging him to stop at the Ramsey pits to take on water, mend a broken petrol pipe and bandage the water pipe. Having fallen back to fourth place, he

recovered to win by a mere 5 seconds from Ray Abbott (Rudge).

The unfortunate Abbott lost the victory when he overshot the last corner, which was then at Parkfield, as in the early days of the Mountain circuit the course was not quite as it is today. (The Signpost Corner to Governor's Bridge section was not used until 1920.) He is pictured here finishing the race at the "Grand Stand" after Bray Hill. (See the pamphlet "50 Years ago: The 2 Day Senior TT Race" by George Stevens published in June 1963 and reprinted from "Yowl", the Scott O.C. Journal.)

Alfie Alexander, third finisher in 1913's Senior TT, at Cruikshanks Corner, Ramsey. Check out the dust. Frank Applebee, the winner of the 1912 Senior on a Scott and the managing director of Godfreys Ltd, the London motorcycle distributors, explained "As far as I can remember there was no tar on the roads, except perhaps at Douglas. Dust was our main problem; the dust and the general roughness of the course made the race a terrific strain for the competitors - a great physical endurance test. At the end of a race many competitors had to be lifted from their machines and held up. A rider was considered amazingly fresh if he could stand at all."
(Walter Radcliffe collection)

For 1914, there were some changes: safety helmets became compulsory, the start was moved to the top of Bray Hill and there was just the one set of refuelling pits, on the school side at Parkfield Corner. The races were booming with 35 different makes of machine entered and no fewer than 30 manufacturer entries. Whereas the 1913 two-stroke Scott was externally similar to the production models, for the 1914 series Scott designed a revolutionary purpose-built racing motorcycle, an example of which survives. Armed with this projectile, Tim Wood, whom we see at Ramsey hairpin, established a lap record of 53.3 mph from his standing start but came to a halt at Union Mills with, supposedly, an oil drenched magneto. For his record lap, Lord Wakefield, the founder of Castrol, awarded him a silver hip flask, which remains in the ownership of his family. (See the pamphlet "50 Years Ago: The 1914 Senior TT Race" by George Stevens published in June 1964.)
(Wood family collection)

Motor Cycling's 1914 TT issue, featuring W. H. Bashall (Douglas) at Keppel Gate, winner of Junior TT, 1912.

When the series resumed in 1920, the course was re-structured, going on from Cronk-ny-Mona to Signpost, Bedstead, the Nook and Governor's Bridge. The start and finish line moved to the Glencrutchery Road, with a grandstand being erected on the Noble's Park side. We see the famous scoreboard, with its individual rider clock-face indicator dials, opposite the new grandstand. Boy scouts moved the finger to the appropriate position, responding to marshals reporting the passage of each rider on the newly-laid telephone line round the circuit. The rider is P. Pike on his 250 cc Levis, starting the Junior TT of 1921 - the 250 cc machines enjoyed their own class within the 350 cc race, competing for "The Motor Cycle" trophy. Use a magnifying glass and spot the trophies to the immediate left of the box.

Harold Petty, Coulson, 1921 Junior TT, changing his tube, through "mist on the Mountain".

Second in the 1921 Junior race astride his AJS, two days later Howard Davies rode the same 350 cc machine to victory in the Senior TT for 500 cc bikes - "the results were received with pardonable incredulity" recorded "The Motor Cycle." Interestingly, his victory at record speed (54.5 mph over six laps of the 37 miles of the new course) prompted claims that the bikes were too fast for the course and that capacity should be limited to 350 cc - nothing changes! Davies (2) is seen leading the Manx star Tom Sheard (9th on H. B. Mylchreest's privately owned Sunbeam) at Braddan Bridge. Sheard was the first Manxman to win a TT, with victories in the Junior in 1922 (AJS) and the Senior in the following year (Douglas). (See "T. M. Sheard: The Modest Manxman" written and published by his granddaughter Ruth Sheard in 2006).

(ex Murray's Museum)

Howard Davies (2) leading J. W. Moffat (Scott, 15, 22nd finisher) at Ballacraine, Senior TT, 1921. Four years later Davies made history by riding his own product to success when he won the Senior TT on the 500 cc H.R.D. - to improve on his runner-up spot on the 350 cc version in the Junior race.

(ex Murray's Museum)

W. H. Hadfield, 500 cc Norton at Creg ny Baa, in the Senior TT, 1921.

(ex *Murray's Museum*)

The legendary Stanley Woods at the Bungalow (at 31 miles), Cotton, Junior TT, 1922 - just having crossed the line of the Snaefell Railway. He finished 5th. With ten TT victories, from the 1923 Junior (Cotton) to the 1939 Junior (Velocette), Woods held the record number of wins until overtaken by Mike Hailwood in 1967. (See "Stanley Woods: A short biography" by W. F. McCleery, published in 1987 by the Ulster Folk and Transport Museum, ISBN 0 902588 25 7.)

The larger-than-life character Freddie Dixon, Indian, at Governor's Bridge, Senior TT, 1922. (See "F.W.Dixon. 'Flying Freddie' 1892-1956" published by Stockton on Tees Borough Council Museum Service in 1986 to mark the 30th anniversary of the death of the outstanding racer and engineer who was born in the town.)

(ex Murray's Museum)

An unidentified rider shoots a quick glance at the camera at Ballig Bridge (after 8 miles, just beyond Ballacraine), probably 1922.
(ex Murray's Museum)

Freddie Dixon, Douglas, leaps Ballig Bridge in the Senior TT of 1924 in which he finished third and set the fastest lap. Freddie was a sidecar exponent and won the 1923 Sidecar TT with the famous Douglas banking sidecar which he designed - the chair could be raised or lowered to suit the bends, and it featured an experimental front disc brake. With his victory (H.R.D.) in the Junior TT of 1927, he became the first man to win two-wheeled and three-wheeled TT races.

He retired from motorcycle racing in 1928 and commenced a car racing career in 1932; he won the Mannin Beg race in the Isle of Man in 1933, took third place in the Le Mans 24 Hours race in the following year and won the Ulster TT in both 1935 and 1936.

(ex Murray's Museum)

A classic shot of Ballig Bridge. Until demolished in the mid-1930s, the bridge was as renowned as Ballaugh for launching the competitors, and it incorporated an S bend for good measure.

IN THE 20's WEIGHING-IN MEANT WHAT IT SAID FOR MACHINE (AND I THINK RIDERS) WERE WEIGHED.

When the "weigh-in" was just that - to ensure that the weight limits stipulated in the regulations were complied with. The official in the natty plus fours, complete with cap, is Sam Huggett, sometime Secretary of the ACU and Clerk of the Course. The photo is probably of 1925 vintage. *(ex Murray's Museum)*

W. T. Lord (Grindlay Peerless), Lightweight TT, 1925, in Parliament Square, before the construction of the version of the Town Hall which featured as the backcloth of so many famous TT shots - see, for example, Mike Hailwood and his Honda six shown subsequently.   *(Walter Radcliffe collection)*

Harold Willis, 350 cc Velocette, pictured at Ballaugh Bridge, riding to second place in the Junior TT of 1928 - beaten only by the ex-Canadian RFC pilot Alec Bennett. Willis joined the Velocette design staff and was responsible for the likes of the blown Roarer, which Stanley Woods tested during practice for the 1939 races. (See "Velocette: Technical Excellence Exemplified" by Ivan Rhodes, ISBN 0-7603-1693-7)

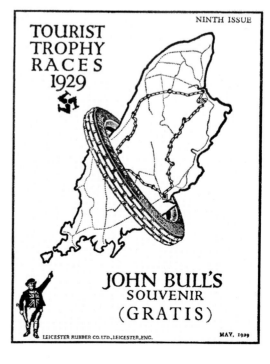

Two shots of Jimmie Guthrie negotiating classic corners as he rides to victory in the 1934 Junior TT; the first is at Creg ny Baa. . .

. . . and the second, just down the road at Hillberry. Guthrie was arguably Britain's foremost rider of the 1930s, with four European titles and six TT successes. His memorial on the Mountain marks the spot at which he retired in his final TT, the Senior of 1937. Other memorials are the Guthrie Stone, erected in 1939 at the scene of his fatal accident at the Sachsenring in the German GP of 1937, and the statue in Wilton Park, Hawick, his home town, near the local museum which features a display of Guthrie memorabilia. (See "Jimmie Guthrie: Hawick's Racing Legend", a booklet published by the Hawick Archaeological Society in 1997)

(Keig collection)

Stanley Woods (Moto Guzzi) rounds Governor's Bridge in the course of winning one of the most exciting TT races ever - the Senior TT of 1935, when he beat the Norton team leader Jimmie Guthrie by a mere four seconds. Woods effectively outwitted Joe Craig, the Norton team manager. Guthrie was number one and began the seventh and final lap with a lead of almost half a minute, over Woods, number thirty. Craig, thinking that the race was in the bag, sent a signal to Ramsey telling Guthrie to ride conservatively to ensure a finish. But, as Guthrie deliberately slowed, the Irishman over-revved the Mandello marque's vee-twin around the final tour and, as he picked up precious seconds, it was too late for Craig to warn his team leader of the threat. With a record lap, Woods snatched a famous victory.

Excelsior-mounted H. G. Tyrell Smith plunges down Bray Hill riding to second place in the Lightweight TT, 1936, behind Bob Foster (New Imperial). He gained eight podium positions, of which one was a victory - the 1930 Junior on a Rudge.

Ginger Wood, 250 cc Excelsior, Parliament Square, Lightweight TT, 1937. He was runner-up to Moto Guzzi's "Black Devil" Omobono Tenni, a result which he repeated in the 1938 race, being beaten then by Ewald Kluge (D.K.W.).

Tenni's victory, achieved by "riding with a crazy abandon which created doubts about his finishing in one piece" (according to "The Motor Cycle"), was the first by an Italian rider on an Italian bike. He was so thrilled by his success that he named his son Titi. Names were evidently a speciality in the Tenni household; he was christened Tommaso but childhood buddies called him Omobono and the nickname stuck, so much so that even his children did not know his name and simply called him Tenni.

Racer and journalist Vic Willoughby was fond of recounting the tale that the raucous sound of the split single Deeks plummeting flat out down Bray Hill could be heard 60 miles away on the English coast. A nice story! A shot from the 1937 Lightweight TT: Siegfried Wunsche, on the 250 cc version, on the Mountain. He finished in 5th place. His best TT result was third place in the 1953 Lightweight race, still with D.K.W. (See "Siegfried Wunsche" by Arne A. Jorgensen, ISBN 3-00-012713-5, available via Mike Jordan at www.motorrennsportarchiv.de)

An absolutely wonderful shot of Freddie Frith at the top of Bray Hill. 500 cc Norton, Senior TT, 1938. He was the third man home. For Norton, he won the Junior in 1936 and the Senior in the following year, when, dicing with Stanley Woods, he became the first man to lap the Mountain at over 90 mph. Following the War, he took the Junior in both 1948 and 1949 astride Velocette machines, as well as the inaugural 350 cc world title.

(ex Lockett)

En route to winning the 1938 Senior, Harold Daniell airborne on Quarter Bridge Road. He repeated his Senior TT success for the works Norton team in 1947 and 1949. Daniell was considered too short-sighted to join the army as a despatch rider.

Programme for the Senior TT, 1938.

Works man Bill Doran takes his 350 cc A.J.S. round Quarter Bridge, Junior TT, 1949. *(ex Lockett)*

Norton teamsters Artie Bell (64) and Johnny Lockett (35) howl up the Cronk y Voddy straight, Junior TT, 1950. Bell won; Lockett was sixth. *(ex Lockett)*

Senior TT, 1950: Bob Foster (Moto Guzzi) trails Norton teamster Johnny Lockett (who finished in third place) as they leave Ramsey. The race saw Geoff Duke (Norton) record the first of his five TT victories. *(ex Lockett)*

The riders await the start of the Junior TT, 1951. Jack Brett (Norton, 5), near the camera, finished in third place behind Duke and Lockett. Yorkshireman Brett's best TT result was second place in the 1953 Senior. Brother Charlie also enjoyed a TT career, from 1937 to 1951, and was a specialist at his local circuits, Scarborough and Esholt. But Charlie subsequently achieved minor celebrity status via his ownership of Brett's fish and chip shop in Headingley, Leeds, a favoured haunt of test cricketers for many years.

(ex Lockett)

A rarely photographed section of the course: Pear Tree Cottage, Appledene.

Privateer Ranson goes through Cronk ny Mona, between Hillberry and Signpost Corner, Senior TT, 1951. He finished in 26th place on his 358 cc AJS.   *(Ranson archive)*

Johnny Lockett (Norton) on what became known as Ago's Leap, in the Senior TT, 1951. In what was to be his final TT race, he suffered the disappointment of a chain breaking while holding second place on the last lap, behind the peerless Duke.

(ex Lockett)

A shot of Ray Amm astride the 500 cc Norton at Keppel Gate (- a gate across the Mountain Road near Kate's Cottage which marked a boundary -) displaying his customary lurid style during the 1954 Senior TT which was held in torrential rain. After two laps, the organisers decided to stop the race at the end of the fourth, by which time sufficient miles would have been covered to qualify for world championship points. But they omitted to notify the team managers or pit attendants of their decision.

Geoff Duke (Gilera) led for two laps but as the weather worsened he slackened the pace. He fell behind Amm on lap three, at the end of which he pitted and thereby lost even more time. By contrast, Amm went straight through non-stop, as his Norton was fitted with pannier tanks. Duke could

Programme for the 1953 races.

not recover the lost time and was still a minute adrift at the end of the fourth lap when the chequered flag fell - by which time bright sunshine had broken through. Gilera's team manager, Piero Taruffi, protested, as did others who had pitted, but after two hours of deliberation the stewards upheld the result. The commonly held view was that Amm was the only rider who was really trying in the atrocious conditions, and C. H. Wood movie film shows the Rhodesian ace employing speedway-style tactics all round the course. "He was simply prepared to take more risks than I was", explained Duke.

The Sidecar TT was re-introduced in 1954 over the Clypse course (so called because it circled the Clypse reservoir) of almost 11 miles. After the start, the Clypse turned right before Bray Hill, at Parkfield Corner, then it turned right again at Willaston Corner, and went to Creg ny Baa, but in the "reverse" direction. At the Creg, the new course took the right fork to Ballacoar, with a sharp right-hander taking it down to the main Douglas-Laxey road. In Onchan, the course turned right to Signpost Corner and then back to the Glencrutchery Road.

Second place man Fritz Hillebrand (BMW) leads Pip Harris (Norton) through Onchan. Hillebrand won the TT in both 1956 and 1957 and the world title in the latter year, when he was killed in a crash at the Bilbao international meeting at the end of August.

1957 at Signpost; under the eye of the law, Geoff Duke, nursing his injuries suffered at the Imola Gold Cup meeting, oversees Bob McIntyre and mechanic Luigi Colombo pushing Bob Brown's 350 cc Gilera "quattro". It has often been written that McIntyre replaced Duke in the Gilera team following the latter's injury at Imola; in fact McIntyre had signed for Gilera at the beginning of the season and, by the time of the TT, had already ridden for the Arcore factory's squad at both Imola and Hockenheim. It was the Australian Brown who replaced Duke at the TT. (See the definitive "Gilera Quattro" ISBN 88-86184-00-X, written by Sandro Colombo, Gilera's race shop chief engineer in the early 1950s, and Osprey's "Gilera Road Racers", ISBN 0-85045-675-4).

Runner-up in the Senior of 1957, reigning 500 cc world champion John Surtees with Nello Pagani. The weather forecast for the race was for blustery conditions so Surtees opted to ride without a dustbin fairing. Not for the first time, the forecasters were confounded as the race was held in perfect Manx weather. A 10 mph disadvantage on the fast sections of the course did not help the Gallarate bike's cause. (See the autobiography "John Surtees: world champion", ISBN 0-905138-73-2)

But in truth it is difficult to believe that any rider could have held McIntyre at the time. Geoff Duke maintained that the Scot could do things with the Gilera which he could only dream of. No apologies for using this famous photo of the Senior TT; it captures the determination of the Flying Scot who broke the Magic Ton on his second lap - of the eight, in honour of the Golden Jubilee. McIntyre related that, as he passed the Guthrie Memorial, he would usually ask the spirit of his countryman to hasten his passage; but, as an exception, in this particular race, such was his dominance and fear of breaking down, that he hoped that Jimmie would slow him down. And, indeed, his Gilera colleagues Duke and Armstrong were frantically signalling to him to ease off.

(*Racing Photos IOM*)

Three great riders: Sammy Miller (28, Ducati), Romolo Ferri (6, Ducati) and Tarquinio Provini (8, MV) at Parkfield Corner, Clypse, 125 cc TT, 1958. Ferri finished in second place behind Carlo Ubbiali (MV). Before signing for Ducati, he had ridden for the Lambretta, Mondial and Gilera factory teams.
(Walter Radcliffe Collection)

Forever associated with Norton and Gilera, Geoff Duke and his great rival Umberto Masetti were probably the sport's first superstars. At the end of his career, Duke enjoyed works rides with both BMW and Benelli. Here we see him on Bray Hill aboard the Munich factory's twin cylinder model in the Senior TT of 1958, from which he retired. (See his autobiography "Geoff Duke: In pursuit of perfection" ISBN 0-85045-838-2) *(Racing Photos IOM)*

1959 and two Clypse circuit scenes "in the country" after the Creg, approaching Ballacoar: Runner-up Carlo Ubbiali (winner of 5 TT races and 9 world titles, thanks to MV and Mondial - see "Rimettersi in Moto" by Gianni Perrone and Jolanda Croesi, a history of Mondial, ISBN 88-7911-229-5) 250 cc MV, Lightweight TT . . .

. . . and the Sidecar TT. 1959 was the final year for the Clypse course, which had hosted sidecar, 125 cc and 250 cc races.

Although greeted with some amusement by the fans, Honda's first appearance in the TT in 1959 was rewarded by the Manufacturer's Team Prize in the 125 cc race. Here we see Giichi Suzuki passing Mathers paper shop in Onchan on his way to 7th place. (See "Honda Racers in the Golden Age" by Mick Woollett, ISBN 4-87366-063-7) *(Walter Radcliffe collection)*

In the same race, the winner, MV star Tarquinio Provini, at the Manx Arms, Onchan. For good measure, Provini doubled up by taking the 250 cc event. However, in doing so he incurred the wrath of his masters. The Agusta family's matriarch, Countess Giuseppina, had decreed that Carlo Ubbiali should win the 250 cc world title. For the race, Mike Hailwood on his private ex-works Mondial upset the Gallarate squad's plans by dicing with them and team orders went out of the window. But the Mondial challenge petered out went out with ignition trouble at Brandish on the penultimate lap, leaving Ubbiali ahead of Provini. Team manger Nello Pagani duly put out the pit board ordering his riders to hold station. Provini simply ignored the instruction and won by half a second. Needless to say, "Old Elbows" was out of a job at the end of the season!

Dickie Dale (BMW) and runner-up Alastair King (Norton), at Barregarrow, Senior TT, 1959. The winner of the Lightweight Manx GP in 1948, Dale enjoyed works rides with a host of teams such as Gilera, Moto Guzzi, MV Agusta and Benelli. King, Bob McIntyre's fellow member of Glasgow's Mercury Club and travelling companion, won the Clubman's Senior TT in 1954 and the 350 cc Formula One event in 1959. Devastated by McIntyre's death following an accident at Oulton Park in 1962, King instantly retired from the sport. One TT week, he turned up at Charlie Murray's with two of Mac's helmets; one was that worn at Assen when McIntyre crashed the Gilera in the Dutch TT in 1957; King donated it for display in Murray's museum. The other was that worn at Oulton Park; King walked out and returned some time later, with tears in his eyes, telling Charlie Murray that he had buried it and that his friend was now at rest.

A youthful Mike Hailwood with his Ecurie Sportive 500 cc Norton in the paddock before the 1959 Senior TT. (See "Mike Hailwood: A motorcycle racing legend" by Mick Woollett, ISBN 1 85960 648 2)

A classic scene: P.J. Millard (Norton) sweeps through Braddan Bridge, Sidecar TT, 1960. The teas, sandwiches and cakes on offer from the church hall are a celebrated feature of race days - a throwback to days gone by. Spectating from the benches, whether in the old churchyard or in the new, watching superbikes hurtle past, is a "must" for the visitor - completely surreal. *(Walter Radcliffe collection)*

John Surtees, 500 cc MV, riding to win his sixth and final TT, the Senior of 1960, passing Ladi Richter's burning Norton at Waterworks Corner. (See "Moto MV" by Mario Colombo and Roberto Patrignani, ISBN 88-7672-012-X, Italian text.)

(Walter Radcliffe collection)

Derek Minter riding to victory in the 1962 Lightweight TT, coming out of Governor's Bridge dip. Minter was entered on a year old "four" by the Honda importers, Hondis Limited, as a second-string rider to support the full works squad. McIntyre was the white-hot favourite thanks to his performance in 1961 when he set a 250 cc lap record which was faster than the 350 cc record. ("My 250 cc bike is faster than my Junior bike and that's faster than my 500 cc bike," he only half-jokingly said of his Honda, Bianchi and Norton). Sure enough, Mac led convincingly at the end of lap one but, to the dismay of his legion of fans, retired at Barregarrow next time around. It was then that, unbeknown to the watching crowds, the political drama started. Before the race, the Honda management had ditched the team orders for McIntyre, Phillis and Redman which were usually to apply in the GPs for that season. But Minter, who was at the top of his form and was generally held to be the world's leading rider in 1962, was told that he was expected to let the works boys win. Redman (whom Honda had planned should take the world title in the class) inherited the lead but was slowed by misfiring and a loose petrol-filler cap. Minter did not back off and rode to his solitary TT success, with Redman and Phillis in second and third.. Far from being pleased by his success, the Honda management was livid, so the "King of Brands" sacrificed his chance of a lucrative contract with the Japanese giant.

1962

INTERNATIONAL TOURIST TROPHY

Programme of Presentation

The Lightweight (250 c.c.) and Sidecar T.T. Races

THE VILLA MARINA : DOUGLAS

9 p.m. MONDAY, 4th JUNE

One of the TT's great characters, Florian Camathias with Alfred Herzig in the chair during practice for the 1964 Sidecar TT. Stories abound - how about the time his van broke down en route to the Island so he packed his luggage onto the platform of his BMW race outfit and rode it to the Liverpool boat? Or when, being very short-sighted, he mistook Reg Armstrong's niece's baby for a doll and threw the package across the pub? Or his early morning unofficial practice sessions on open roads?

Winner of the 1963 race with his FCS (powered by a BMW cared for by Helmut Fath), Camathias sought a power-plant to enable him to challenge for the world title which had so far eluded him. His Italian-speaking wife visited Commendatore Gilera in Arcore and managed to secure one of the ex-Duke 500 cc engines for the 1964 campaign.

The Swiss pairing arrived at Ramsey on lap one with a lead of five seconds over Deubel. Despite the loss of fourth gear, he maintained the lead until he overshot at Signpost, handing Deubel a narrow lead. Sadly, fuel starvation beset the Gilera on the third and final lap, and Deubel had made up the thirty seconds starting differential by Ramsey. Then the Italian multi died at Kate's Cottage, and the German champion swept past to take the chequered flag.

Camathias stopped to inspect the engine and set off again only to run into a bank, damaging the screen and the long-suffering Herzig. The pair eventually coasted downhill and pushed in accompanied by stupendous applause to finish in 15th place and take the final bronze replica.

The 50 cc machines were introduced to the world championship series and the TT in 1962. Suzuki was the dominant marque, with its two-stroke machines being perfected by Ernst Degner following his defection from MZ in 1961. Incidentally, he did not defect to Japan as is so often written; he obtained a West German passport. In the early years, Suzuki's closest challenger in the 50 cc class was Kreidler which in 1964 added Taveri and Provini to Anscheidt in its squad. Here we see Provini riding to 8th place on the 12 speed tiddler.

On leaving MV, he realised that he was happiest as a lone wolf and passed into Morini service for four seasons. When the 250 cc Morini (traditionally but inaccurately dubbed "the world's fastest single") was getting long in the tooth, he opted for multi cylinder power and, forsaking offers from Japan, joined Benelli in 1964. It was on a Benelli that he crashed heavily near Ballaugh in practice for the 1966 series. At the time, marshal points were spread out over large distances and he lay by the side of the road for almost half-an-hour before being attended to.

The popular theory was that he had been caught out by the early morning sun but years later he offered a bizarre explanation. He claimed that a piston had broken during the previous evening's practice run and that, as the race machine had not yet arrived from Italy, the conrod was sawn through to make the hack serviceable; next morning the remaining metal from the conrod heated up, exploded and locked the engine.

Whatever the truth of the incident, Provini lay in hospitals for many months and was warned that he would never walked again. He was determined to prove the doctors wrong and did so, eventually making a full recovery, although he suffered pain for the rest of his life. He developed the Protar model series and remained involved in the classic scene, returning to parade in the Isle of Man in 1985 and participating in revivals in Italy.

Programme for the 1964 races.

Another "rebel": Phil Read. Winner of the Senior Manx GP in 1960, Read established his credentials with victory in the Junior TT of 1961. An unhappy experience with Scuderia Duke in 1963 astride the tired and under-financed Gileras was nevertheless followed by a contract with Yamaha. We see him round Quarter Bridge in the Lightweight TT of 1964; although he and his two-stroke twin were the fastest combination, he retired.

Max Deubel and Emil Horner (BMW) pictured in 1965. Deubel was unable to get to grips with the "kneelers" which his competitors were using, but it did him little harm - he won the TT in 1961, 1964 and 1965 and the world title from 1961 to 1964 inclusive.

Phil Read unexpectedly gave the Yamaha marque its first TT win in the Ultra-Lightweight of 1965. Starting ten seconds behind Honda's star turn Taveri on the four-stroke "four", he caught and passed him. Although re-passed by the Swiss world champion, he sat on his tail for the final lap to clinch the first of his eight TT wins. Pictured in that race we see Luigi Taveri on Bray Hill. Taveri had enjoyed works rides with MV, MZ and Ducati but it was not until he joined Honda that he struck gold, winning the 125 cc race in 1962 and 1964, and the 50 cc event in 1965.

Honda's Rhodesian team leader Jim Redman aboard the 350 cc "four" on which he completed his consecutive "triple double" of 250 cc and 350 cc wins in 1965. It turned out to be his final TT race. A crash in the Belgian GP on the new 500 cc Honda "four" put him out for the rest of the 1966 season and he missed the TT which had been delayed to August because of the seamen's strike. He then retired from the sport but in recent years has been a familiar figure on the classic scene and often returns to the TT.

Giacomo Agostini, on the new 350 cc MV "three", at Ballaugh Bridge, riding in his first TT, the 1965 Junior, in which he finished third behind Redman (Honda) and Read (Yamaha).

Mike Hailwood, 500 cc MV Agusta, en route to winning the Senior TT, 1965. The race was held in dismal conditions and Mike the Bike's team-mate, Agostini, dropped his "quattro" at Sarah's Cottage on the second lap. Next time around and Hailwood repeated the trick, falling off beneath Ago's gaze. But Hailwood picked up his "fire engine", kicked the handlebars straight and re-started (in the "right direction" dutifully reported "Motor Cycle" - the magazine dropped the "The" in May 1962) complete with flattened exhaust megaphones, a shattered windscreen and a bent clutch lever, to record a famous victory. It subsequently emerged that Hailwood had in fact bump started the beast downhill - but in the wrong direction, for which he should have been disqualified. (*Racing Photos IOM*).

Helmut Fath with his home-brewed URS four cylinder outfit, Parliament Square, Sidecar TT, 1967. Fath won the TT and the world title in 1960 with BMW power. However, in April 1961, he crashed in the Eifelrennen meeting at the Nurburgring; he sustained serious injuries and his passenger Alfred Wohlgemuth lost his life. For some time, as he recovered full health Fath contented himself with tuning duties. He eventually returned to the tracks with the URS and recovered the world title in 1968.

Fred Hanks (BSA) leads Attenberger (BMW) into Parliament Square, Sidecar TT 1967.

Geoff Davison won the Lightweight TT in 1922 and as his TT career came to a conclusion he established "The TT Special" in 1927 - which at its peak gave almost instant reports of practice and then each day's racing. Davison also wrote, in 1947, the sought-after "The Story of the TT- A book for Motor Cyclists and all others who believe that motor cycle road racing is the finest sport on earth". Following Davison's death in 1966, Fred Hanks took over the newspaper, which sadly folded in 1985. However, to some extent, the void has been filled in recent years by the welcome appearance of "TT News", which (although not a same day service) offers a review of practice and two race week issues. It follows the spirit of "The TT Special" by offering not simply reports and results but also news items, gossip, interviews, adverts and tales of races in, and heroes of, years past.

With the old Town Hall as the backdrop, Mike Hailwood takes the fabulous 250 cc Honda six through Parliament Square, Lightweight TT, 1967.

Bill Ivy being interviewed by Murray Walker. Ivy took two TT victories for Yamaha but it was actually a second place which brought him the most headlines. The 1968 Ultra-Lightweight race will be remembered for him establishing the first 100 mph lap on a 125 cc machine. Then, with a comfortable lead, he pointedly stopped at the Creg to ask the spectators the whereabouts of team-mate Read; on re-starting, Ivy dutifully obeyed instructions by taking second place. Of course, later that season, Read chose to ignore team orders and took what should have been Ivy's 250 cc world title.

Murray Walker's father, Graham, won the 1931 Lightweight TT for Rudge; he subsequently became the editor of "Motor Cycling". In 1927, the first BBC commentary of the races was given by Canon B.H. Davies (the famous "Ixion", renowned contributor to "The Motor Cycle" and author of the classic book "Motor Cycle Cavalcade" in 1950). Graham Walker took over the microphone in 1934 and broadcast the TT over the airwaves for many years.

And let us remember Peter Kneale, the "Voice of the TT", who commentated on the races from 1965 until 2000. Who can ever forget his welcome to race-goers on the Saturday of race week when (with luck), from his commentary perch at the grandstand, he would report that "the sun is glistening on the fairings", and his customary farewell six days later when, the races over, he would seek to cheer up his listeners by reminding us that we had only fifty weeks to go before we could start all over again.

A shot of the Douglas Bay Hotel, home to many visiting works teams, with team manager Innocenzo Nardi Dei, Mimo Benelli (one of six brothers who together, under the auspices of their widowed mother, established the Benelli firm in Pesaro) and Renzo Pasolini astride a 350 cc Benelli, 1968.

After the unusual "Le Mans" start, Peter Darvill (Honda) and Hans-Otto Butenuth (BMW) lead the 750 cc pack down Bray Hill; Production TT, 1971.

A poignant shot of Morbidelli's Gilberto Parlotti entering Parliament Square, in the 125 cc TT of 1972. The race was held in atrocious conditions and the Italian star crashed in the mist on the Mountain, with fatal consequences. His close friend Giacomo Agostini was devastated and had to be talked into riding in the afternoon's Senior TT. But Ago and the MV team would never return.

ISLE OF MAN
TOURIST
TROPHY RACES

Isle of Man Post Office Authority
OFFICIAL FIRST DAY COVER

A hero of the 1970s, Mick Grant takes the watercooled three cylinder 500 cc Kawasaki round Ramsey hairpin, Senior TT, 1975. Grant will be forever associated with the 750 cc Green Meanie on which he set a series of record laps and won the Classic TT in 1977 and 1978. He was however a party to one of the TT's most controversial incidents: at the end of the Formula One TT of 1980, when he narrowly beat Crosby, as Grant arrived back in the victory bay he bashed his Honda's tank, notionally in his unrestrained delight. The Suzuki squad suspected that the tank had been oversize and that there had been method in the Yorkshireman's madness but the result stood. There could have been no lasting hard feelings as, in the following year, Grant joined the New Zealander in the Suzuki team.

Perhaps the definitive racing machine of the late 1970s and the early 1980s was Suzuki's RG 500. We see Pat Hennen at Signpost in the Senior TT of 1978. Hennen was one of the last riders competing in the world championship races who was happy to take on the challenge of the Mountain course - as the TT lost its world title status after the 1976 races. Unfortunately, Hennen's career was ended by a heavy crash in this race.

Graeme Crosby (Suzuki RG 500) takes Ballaugh Bridge in practice for the Senior of 1980, which was to be the first of his three victories (all for the works Suzuki squad) in the New Zealander's short but brilliant TT career.

His other two successes were laced with controversy. He won the Formula One race on the opening Saturday of 1981 TT week when, having missed his allotted starting slot, he was obliged to start from the back of the grid, without any credit for the starting delay. The race was originally awarded to his Honda rival, Ron Haslam. After a complaint by Suzuki, Crosby was credited with the lost time, which gave him the win.

As a criticism against that decision in particular and what was regarded as antiquated organisation in general, the Honda squad (Dunlop, George and Haslam) appeared for Friday's Classic TT decked out in black leathers and black paintwork on their steeds. The one-two of Suzuki's Crosby and Grant put Honda into the shade.

During practice week, Roger Marshall with Joey Dunlop's 850 cc Honda, riding to the team's garage in the back streets of Douglas, 1983. He took his bike to fourth place in the Formula One TT. Marshall registered a healthy number of podium finishes but a win eluded him.

Few riders could hold Joey Dunlop in the 1980s; Rob McElnea was one of the few, winning both the Senior and Classic races in 1984. We see him here on the 500 cc Heron Suzuki at Tower Bends in the Senior race. McElnea left the TT to pursue a successful career in GP racing and subsequently became, and remains, a team manager for Yamaha.

Con Law (350 cc Yamaha) pictured at Tower Bends, in the Formula Two race of 1985. Irishman Law won the Junior 250 cc race in 1982 on a Waddon Ehrlich and in the following year's virtually unchallenged victory in the same event he became the first man to take a 250 cc machine round at over 110 mph. In doing so, he gave Dr Joe Ehrlich's EMC marque its first TT success. Law is still involved in the sport, acting as a travelling marshal in the Irish road races and parading at the TT and the Spa Bikers' Classics meetings.

Roberto Patrignani has enjoyed a unique motorcycling career. In his younger days, he competed in the Giro d'Italia and a range of international events from Daytona to the TT in 1960 and 1961. He passed to journalism, rode a scooter from Milan to Tokyo in 1964 and followed up that marathon feat with rides across Africa, the USA and South America. He was part of the 50 cc Garelli and V7 Moto Guzzi world record-breaking squads in the 1960s, team manager for Suzuki Europa (with his number one rider, Jack Findlay, winning the Senior TT in 1973) and p.r. man for Guzzi and Garelli. He returned to race in the TT in 1989 and is seen here getting off the line starting the Production TT on his RC30 Honda, which he retains to this day in his garage in Mandello del Lario. He told the story of the 1989 venture in his book "Ti portero a Bray Hill". His TT swansong came in 1999 when he practiced for the Junior aboard a 600 cc Honda, as the basis of a number of features for Italian magazines. He has participated in the Lap of Honour on many occasions. *(Patrignani collection).*

Trevor Nation, on the rotary Norton, Quarter Bridge, Senior TT, 1989. Simon Buckmaster, Nation, Steve Cull and Robert Dunlop all campaigned Nortons with distinction but it was Steve Hislop who took the bike to a famous victory in the Senior TT of 1992.

One of the TT greats, Steve Hislop at Signpost Corner in the Senior TT of 1991. He was riding the jewel-like 750 cc RVF Honda, originally built for the world endurance championship; he beat the sister bike twice, ridden by Carl Fogarty in the Formula One race and then by Joey Dunlop in the Senior. With eleven victories, his final ride over the Mountain was on the then new Honda RC45 in the 1994 Senior, whereafter he concentrated on British superbike racing.

Ian Lougher (58), seen at the end of Sulby Straight, in the 125 cc event of 1992, had established himself as a leading lightweight rider with his victory in the Junior race of 1990 (technically for 350 cc machines but for quarter litre bikes in reality), when he beat hot favourite Steve Hislop setting lap and race records into the bargain. By the turn of the Millennium, he had also become a contender in the larger capacity classes, riding for the TAS Suzuki squad, an ex-Colin Edwards Honda SP02 for Honda Britain in 2003, and then Fireblades for Mark Johns, the DMRR squad and Paul Bird in 2006. The Ulster-based Welshman had won 7 TTs by the end of the 2006 series but a sought-after superbike TT win eluded him.

Re-fuelling in the Supersport 600 cc race of 1992, Geoff Cannell, long-time commentator and pits link-man for Manx Radio's race coverage, looks on as Honda's team manager Neil Tuxworth organises Phillip McCallen's stop, with Nick Jefferies and Joey Dunlop down the line.

Carl Fogarty on the 750 cc Yamaha in the Formula One TT, 1992. He led the race comfortably only to retire and hand a first TT victory to McCallen. In the Senior race six days later, Fogarty finished a whisker behind Hislop, Norton, in one of the TT's greatest races. He established a lap record of 123.61 mph which endured for seven years. With that, he left the TT, with three wins to his credit, and of course became a WSB champion with Ducati.

John Britten waiting to take his fantastic creation into the scrutineering bay during practice week, 1993. The revolutionary vee-twin machine was to be ridden in the Senior TT by Shaun Harris; it is fair to say that the sight and sound of this wonderful beast enthused commentators and fans alike. (For the story of the remarkable designer, see "John Britten" by Tim Hanna, ISBN 1-877333-08-5, and "Britten Motorcycles" by Felicity Price, ISBN 0-7603-2056-X. See also www.britten.co.nz)

With Fogarty and Hislop missing the TT, the 1993 Formula One race was open to all contenders. At the end of lap one, the Ducati pairing of Robert Dunlop and Mark Farmer, seen at Signpost Corner, had the ascendancy over the Honda squad but the Italian vee-twin bikes soon proved to be fragile, handing victory to Nick Jefferies on the RC30.

Robert Dunlop has enjoyed a sensational career. In winning the Junior Newcomers Manx GP in 1983, he beat Steve Hislop and Ian Lougher. For ten years, he was a leading rider on everything from the ultra-lightweights to rotary Nortons, until his crash in the Formula One TT in 1994 on a Honda RC45 at Ballaugh left him seriously injured. After a lengthy period of recuperation,

he returned to take more TT and international victories on 125 cc machines. Having missed the 2005 season for another operation, he won the North West 200 and collected numerous national victories in 2006.

Britten returned to the Island in 1994, determined to challenge the Honda hegemony. Alas, it was not to be. Mark Farmer aboard the Roberto Crepaldi-owned CR&S Britten crashed the big vee-twin at Black Dub on the Thursday afternoon practice session, possibly trying to keep in touch with Steve Hislop who had just overtaken him aboard the new Honda RC45. John Britten was deeply affected by Farmer's death and was reputed never to have recovered from the trauma.

The second Britten team member, the Kiwi Rob Holden, whom we see here about to start a practice session, decided to concentrate on his Supersport 600 and Ducati Supermono rides and his Britten was set aside as a spare. But then John Britten offered the bike to Jason McEwan, who was part of the Kiwi team competing in the 600 cc class for the Maudes Trophy. McEwan had experience of racing the Britten but, having completed insufficient practice laps with it, he was not allowed to start.

The third member of the Britten squad of 1994, Nick Jefferies, is seen here at Quarter Bridge. John Britten died on 5 September 1995, aged just 45. His team decided to return to the Island in 1996 and the CR&S bike was given the number one plate as a mark of respect. Shaun Harris was re-united with the Britten and took it to an emotional finish in the Senior TT.

The winner of 1990's Senior Manx GP, Simon Beck, Ducati, stops in Ballaugh "for adjustments", practice, 1995.

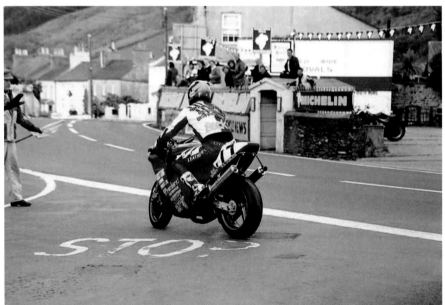

Having sampled the Britten in 1993, two years later Shaun Harris was the pilot of an even more eccentric machine - the 750 cc Suzuki engined, hub-centre-steering Tryphonos, seen here at Quarter Bridge. Witnesses will never forget a practice session when, as he left the line on Glencrutchery Road, the Tryphonos simply spat the New Zealander yards into the air. "It's a beast," was his honest reaction. But the bike had undeniable potential; despite a limited budget and a heavy crash in practice, Harris registered a very creditable 11th place in the Senior TT, 1995. After years of trying, the Kiwi collected two trophies in 2003, in the 600 cc and 1,000 cc Production classes.
(See www.tryphonos.com)

Another eccentric bike, the Yamaha campaigned by Steve Linsdell of Flitwick Motorcycles, in Ballaugh during a practice session in 1995. A seasoned campaigner over the Mountain circuit, Linsdell took second place in the Senior Classic Manx GP in August 2006 aboard the fabulous twin cylinder Paton.

The 1997 Formula One TT and Phillip McCallen (Honda) rounds Signpost Corner.

McCallen recorded eleven wins but his year of grace was 1996 when he became the first, and so far the only, rider to notch four wins in the week, taking the Formula One, Senior, Junior 600cc and Production races.

A member of a famous racing family, Bob Jackson, takes the McAdoo Kawasaki round Signpost Corner, Formula One TT, 1997. In the following year he was robbed of victory in the Senior TT. Having fitted a large tank, he was able to re-fuel just once, as against the two stop strategy for the Honda teamsters Ian Simpson and Michael Rutter. Ironically, he was delayed at the stop by a filler cap problem which effectively cost him the race, as he lost out to Simpson by a few seconds. Bob's illustrious career was brought to an end by an accident in Ireland but he is a keen spectator as brother Alan "Bud" Jackson continues his own successful TT and Manx GP career.

David Jefferies, the only man to win a TT treble three years in a row - 1999, 2000 and 2002. (2001 of course fell victim to foot and mouth) His successes on V&M Yamahas in 1999 and 2000 established him as the man to beat, and he continued his dominance of the event in 2002 when he had switched to Hector and Philip Neill's TAS Suzuki squad. He is pictured here on the 1,000 cc superbike in 2003.

The Jefferies clan is unarguably the TT's most successful family. Allan was runner-up in the Clubman's Senior TT in 1947; son Tony won three races in the early 1970s; younger son Nick won the Formula One TT in 1993; Tony's son David was the lap record holder at the time of his tragic death during practice for the 2003 series.

Pictured at the Gooseneck in 2003 is Jim Moodie on the Triumph in the 600 cc Junior race, when the Triumph squad won the Manufacturers' Team Award with Bruce Anstey taking the victory and Moodie and McGuinness backing him up with 9th and 10th positions. Moodie, one of the decade's leading riders, had a reputation as a determined and professional racer. In his victorious ride in the Singles TT of 1994, the Glaswegian's Yamaha was spewing oil, blinding Robert Holden who complained that his Ducati Supermono was faster but he could not see to get by. In fairness to Moodie, he had caught and passed Holden on the road and could hardly be expected to surrender a cherished TT win without a fight. A "big bike" win eluded the Scot but, on an outdated Honda RC45, he established an outright lap record in 1999. He was therefore less than enamoured when, for the following year, Honda gave him what he regarded as an inadequate Fireblade, leading him to walk out of the team part way through the races. *(Eddy Richardson)*

A shot of Lincolnshire's Guy Martin during his debut at the TT in 2004. The master of Oliver's Mount, Scarborough, Martin seemed on the verge of TT success in 2006 when a sensational practice week on the AIM Yamaha augured well. However, it was followed by a disastrous race week. But, by taking four victories in the Ulster GP in August 2006, Martin established himself at the forefront of the new generation of likely lads, alongside Aussie Cameron Donald and Ian Hutchinson. *(Eddy Richardson)*

The TT debut in 2004 (as seen here) of the 2001 sidecar world champions from Austria, Klaus Klaffenbock and Christian Parzer, gave the class a significant boost. He returned in 2005 and 2006 seeking a win and also supported Martin Finnegan's solo campaign in 2006.

(Eddy Richardson)

The main hall in Murray's Museum at the Bungalow. October 2005 and Peter Murray with the ex-Mike Hailwood 250 cc Mondial of 1957 vintage. Peter's father, Charlie, started the world famous motorcycle museum in Peel, moving to the Bungalow site in the late 1960s. The museum featured an marvellous assortment of motorcycle and memorabilia (such as Bob McIntyre's trophies, courtesy of his daughter Eleanor). Highlights included an ex Hailwood/Taveri type 1960/61 125 cc Honda; the Fruin specials - the two 125 cc twin cam racers and the four cylinder 200 cc two stroke; an ex-Arthur Wheeler Moto Guzzi and so on...

But perhaps the most poignant story concerns an extremely rare works Frera racer of 1923 vintage and a diversion into Manx GP history is called for. When the Amateur TT began in 1923, it was stipulated that there should be no works machines entered. However, the TT star Manxman Tom Sheard, who ran a Douglas marque dealership, somehow secured a works Frera racer from Italy for local lad Ned Brew. Externally, the bike was very similar to the production models and hence the scrutineers voiced no objection. One morning practice, Brew passed through Hillberry, the site of his family home, and waved to his sister standing by the roadside. In doing so, he lost control and crashed. He was carried into his house and later died in hospital. The Frera stayed in the Isle of Man and eventually passed into Murray ownership.

However, at the end of the 2005 season, Peter Murray announced the closure of the museum and the sale of its contents. With help of Steve Griffith (son of John, the author of "Historic Racing Motorcycles" and other landmark books covering famous racing motorcycles, and brother of David, the TT rider), some of the bikes (including the Frera) were disposed of, but Peter simply replaced them with other models. So it was that the museum once more welcomed enthusiasts for the TT and Manx GP fortnights in 2006, never to re-open.

The museum will be sorely missed; no audio-visual display units, no interactive computers, no customer surveys, no website but endless tales of Bobby Mac (the greatest rider ever, in Peter's view), a nip of whisky proffered, a penny in the slot into the symphonion (which prompted the saying "The penny has dropped"), an egg sandwich in the cafe at the rear - great memories for generations of visitors.

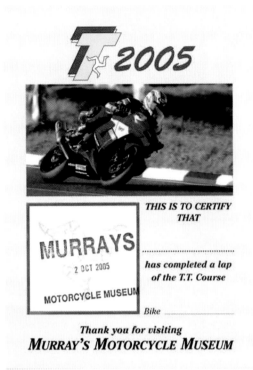

We conclude as we started - at Ballacraine. Appropriately, our final shot is one of the current "King of the Mountain", John McGuinness, seen on his Honda Fireblade in practice for the Superbike TT, 2006. By the end of the fortnight, McGuinness had taken a treble, notched up his eleventh win and left the lap record at 129.451 mph (17m 29.26s).

BIBLIOGRAPHY

Throughout the captions there are references to particular publications, relating to marques or riders, which it is hoped will be of assistance to readers. The following books relate to the history of the TT.

Motocourse History of the Isle of Man Tourist Trophy Races, by Nick Harris, 1990, ISBN 0-905138-71-6

The Isle of Man TT: An Illustrated History 1907-80, by Matthew Freudenberg, 1990, ISBN0 946627 57 6

Steve Hislop's "You couldn't do it now!" by Peter Beighton and Andrew Douglas, 1993, ISBN 1 898363 00 5

The Tourist Trophy: In Old Photographs, by Bill Snelling, 1994, ISBN 0-7509-0635-9

Japanese Riders in the Isle of Man, by Ralph Crellin, 1995, ISBN 0 9527617 0 X

90 Years of TT magic, by Peter Kneale, 1998, ISBN 1 873120 37 0

Classic Images: Isle of Man TT Races, 2001, ISBN 0-953-8357-2-3

TT Mixture, by David Wright, 2003, ISBN 1 901508 07 2

The Magic of the TT, by Mac McDiarmid, 2004, ISBN 1 84425 002 4

Websites:

www.iomtt.com	Official TT website with an extensive historical database and news items.
www.roadracing.com	Latest news of real road racing in the Isle of Man, Ireland and UK.
www.ttra.co.uk	TT Riders' Association.
www.ttsupportersclub.com	The website of the TT Supporters' Club.
www.ttwebsite.com	General TT information site.
www.mcb.net/amulree	Amulree publications and FoTTofinders site.

About the author: Raymond Ainscoe is a contributor to numerous classic bike magazines. He first visited the Isle of Man to watch the TT as a five year old in 1959 and since then has been an ardent fan of the world's greatest road races, as a spectator, sponsor, reporter and participant in the Classic Parades on two occasions. He parades and races classic Gileras over public roads circuits in Belgium and the Netherlands.

About S.C.S.: It is an Isle of Man registered company specialising in all aspects of the building services industry. It remains committed to its domestic customer base, providing a comprehensive service, dealing with plumbing and heating, pools and spas, boilers and servicing, building and electrical work. S.C.S. also has a designated team specialising in commercial activity, having major contracts with the government, the finance sector, and retail and manufacturing services. S.C.S. can be contacted at Ballannette Park, Baldrine, one of the prettiest parts of the Island. Ballannette is a wildlife habitat in natural wetlands which has been developed by S.C.S. so as not to disturb the native and visiting birdlife regularly seen locally. It is open to the public. Website: www.scs.co.im